KNOW YOUR SCIENCE TOOLS

LET'S USE A RULER

DENNIS LIU

PowerKiDS press

Published in 2027 by The Rosen Publishing Group, Inc.
2544 Clinton Street, Buffalo, NY 14224

First Edition

Editor: Noah Riccardi
Book Design: Claire Vanden Branden

Photo Credits: Cover, p. 1 Rohane Hamilton/Shutterstock.com; p. 5 Fadfebrian/Shutterstock.com; p. 7 trindade51/Shutterstock.com; p. 9 Iuliana Cucereavii/Shutterstock.com; p. 11 Mulad Images/Shutterstock.com; p. 13 Okin_Luberto/Shutterstock.com; p. 15 AP Chanel/Shutterstock.com; p. 17 New Africa/Shutterstock.com; p. 19 Rosamar/Shutterstock.com; p. 21 Meng Kongsak/Shutterstock.com.

Cataloging-in-Publication Data
Names: Liu, Dennis.
Title: Let's use a ruler / Dennis Liu.
Description: Buffalo, New York : PowerKids Press, 2027. | Series: Know your science tools | Includes glossary and index.
Identifiers: ISBN 9781499459548 (pbk.) | ISBN 9781499459555 (library bound) | ISBN 9781499459562 (ebook)
Subjects: LCSH: Length measurement--Juvenile literature. | Rulers (Instruments)--Juvenile literature. | Tape measures--Juvenile literature.
Classification: LCC QC102.L58 2027 | DDC 530.8--dc23

Manufactured in China

CPSIA Compliance Information: Batch #QS27PK. For Further Information contact Rosen Publishing, at 1-800-237-9932.

CONTENTS

In Your Hands

You probably have used a ruler in school. Maybe you used it to help you draw straight lines. You might have used one to measure how long something is. You may have measured the distance between two objects. Let's learn about these super science tools!

Inches and Centimeters

Lots of rulers have different **units** of measurement on both edges. One edge shows inches. This unit is mainly used in the United States. The other edge shows centimeters and millimeters. These units belong to the **metric** system. Many countries use the metric system.

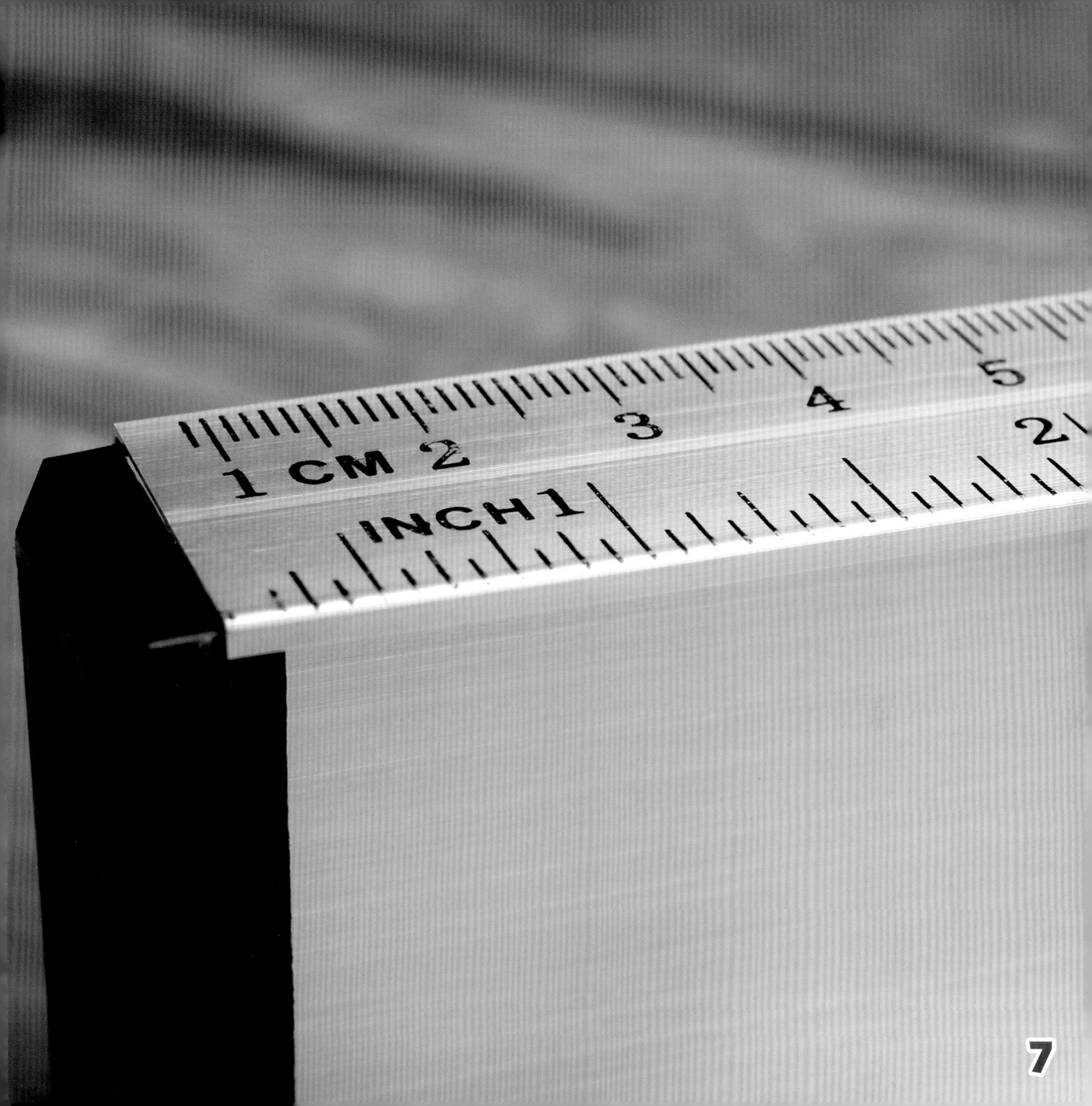
1 CM 2 3 4 5
INCH 1 2

Using a Ruler

Let's measure something in inches. Line up one end of an object with the line at the end of the ruler. Without moving the ruler, look at where the far end of the object lines up with the ruler. That's its length!

25FEET
7.5m

The distance you want to measure might not be a whole number. So you need to use a **fraction**. Ruler marks between whole numbers help you. For example, an object that reaches halfway between 1 and 2 inches is $1\frac{1}{2}$ inches long.

9
10
11
12

Now, let's measure in centimeters. These are on the other side of the ruler. Each mark between centimeters stands for 1 millimeter. Ten millimeters equal 1 centimeter. Centimeters are smaller than inches. Two inches are equal to about five centimeters. The metric system is used a lot in science.

Other Kinds of Ruler

Rulers aren't the only tools we have to measure length. A yardstick is a flat ruler that's 1 yard long. One yard is equal to 3 feet (0.9 m). Calipers are a measuring tool with two moving "legs" and a ruler. The legs fit around the **width** of an object.

A measuring tape can be really long. It's like a long, flat ruler that can roll up. It's good for measuring **circumference**. People also use it to measure how wide rooms are.

Rulers Everywhere!

Measurements are everywhere you look! Truck drivers read measurements to make sure their trucks fit under bridges. Construction workers have to measure things so the parts of buildings fit together. Doctors measure you to see how much you're growing!

13'-8"
SPEED
LIMIT
35

Measure Carefully

A famous saying goes, "measure twice, cut once." That means it's important to measure carefully, then double-check the number. Measuring again can save you from problems that happen because of wrong measurements. True scientists measure twice!

Watts

GLOSSARY

circumference: The distance around the outside of a circle.

fraction: A part of a whole.

metric: Part of a system of measurements based on units such as the liter and meter.

units: Amounts of length, weight, volume, or other measurements.

width: The amount of space from one side of an object to the other.

FOR MORE INFORMATION

BOOKS

Harts, Marie. *Measurement*. Buffalo, NY: Rosen Publishing, 2024.

O'Daly, Anne. *Measuring Distance*. Buffalo, NY: Rosen Publishing, 2024.

WEBSITES

BBC Bitesize: Draw and Measure Accurately
bbc.co.uk/bitesize/articles/zcxy6g8
Learn more about how to use rulers to draw and measure.

Britannica Kids: Metric System
kids.britannica.com/kids/article/metric-system/353458
Find out more about the metric system's importance in science.

INDEX